Island Girl Summer Poetry

Madi Duren

Presentation by *BookLeaf Publishing*

Web: www.bookleafpub.com

E-mail: info@bookleafpub.com

ISBN: 9789363309746

First edition 2024

To Julian Harris, who encouraged me in the process as well as doing the challenge along with me.

Island Girl Gotta Go

Can't pack my suitcase no moa
Da zippah got stuck and I'm stuck
Hea crying on da floor

How come Hawai'i gotta go from me
Whenever I leave to new tings like da mainland
And dat new life aheada me
Real scary
Real new
Real good for dis Island Girl
But she don't wanna go but she don't wanna
stay
But she know she hear da call to go fa fa away
Moses and dem Israelite people
Rushing between God's expansive blue
She reads dat one verse bout how
She's God's precious tool
And I lean back like
"I knew I knew I knew"
I pick my sorry okole up from da ground
Take my two feet up on dat bugga "Suitcase"
And stomp on it

Makin' me feel like one reeaaal proud kine
Island Girl

Bubbles for Thoughts

My thoughts are like bubbles
I can't hold onto bubbles
They'll pop!
My thoughts'll pop
Endless thoughts endless
Explosions blasts bombs endless
Devouring grasping clutching endless
Screaming at the flow
I couldn't hold onto anything
Then
You
Pointed out multitudes of the fantastical aspects
of these bubbles, even with their short life
My bubbles
My thoughts
You helped me see all these beautiful
All my beautiful bubbles!

Tone Over Text

I can't hear your tone over text
So when you sent me that
You had me vexed
What do I send next? What do I do to
Continue what's simply complex?

MY PHONE BUZZED! <3 <3 <3
AAAAA!!! <3 <3 <3
Big inhale!! <3 <3 <3
Ok!! <3 <3 <3
OK it's not you it's an email.
A notification from some big time
Corporate chain– Not your online
Messenger username.
No new information to help me in
My communication with you
No clues or mysteries to piece together so
I can be at peace with you
I'd hope my conscientious thinking would
Be something that'd be pleasing you and if
You were here in front of me I could be
receiving you but you're not and i'm hot
With frustration over the thought that the
Knot of Distance and Time should be united and
then tried in the court of law

Then sent to prison and castrated for screwing
me over like it was their God
Given mission

It has me wrecked.

And I start to suspect
If this interaction was built on respect
And I worry if our complex conversation would
be simply solved if I could hear your
Tone over text.

Nevertheless in my defense I tried to express
myself fully and honestly at the
Expense of not being able to hear your tone

You can find me waiting for you on the
Other side of your phone

HalfHalf

Sliced Specifically
Condemned to Juggle
Mom and Dad Blood
Sent to Befuddling
Scratching Self-Identity:
Asians call me Caucasian
Caucasians swear I'm Asian
"White Bitch"//"Asian delight"
Pulled from one truth
Blinded from my right
to show you
Which I wish you could see
Me under my motherfather skin
Standing in my Real Solid Color
You'll wish I was always seen this way
Yeah man!! I'd admit "same"
But the sun comes up and so do the other colors
saying "You're this way" "You're that way"
and in that time, I go "okokok" when I want to
say
"Go away!!!"

Request from your seed

Don't protect me, Great Wind, push me
Hard and far
Far from being born like a Protected
Nurtured Seeds that grow in rows In
Perfect Conditions No
No No Give me
Give me hale the gust the rain dashing on my
teeth
I want my life to be written in cursive vines
spilling
Stories of a bleeding spirit and my broken bones
holding me upwards as I find
My footing in soft ground and then slipping
down in the mud and crashing on stones
Thrown at unreasonable heights into
unspeakable depths daring death while
Growing
At strange angles
Growing
Fruit fit for angels
Growing God's great winged-roots so that I soar
And stick around at the same time

Legacical Role

I look back at a path so colorful in it's past
That when I turn behind me I see static
uncertainty

The people before me and after me, such
responsibility
Many echoes are carried in the placement of my
feet

If you believe
then you believe
That this legacy
that this legacy
Will go far beyond the static
Will go far beyond the uncertainty
Will go far beyond into horizons
If you believe
Thrust your feet forward

Scary Giant Eye and The Precious Living Gem

MOST PRECIOUS LIVING GEM
LODGED IN SCARY GIANT'S EYE
THE PRECIOUS LIVING GEM SHINES
BRIGHT
LODGED IN SCARY GIANT'S EYE

A TESTAMENT THAT
SCARY GIANT SHINES TOO
THERE IN THE HOLE IS THE LAST
EVIDENCE OF HIS SHINING TRUTH

Different Angles

Dark ember
Your splendor
I surrender on
The stain

Me soul tender
Kiss me tender
I remember on
The Stain

Cup of white light Shakey
window shades still Spit
split the fogs blues Burst
I found Myself
exploding with Stars
asking Myself

Who am I what am I why I am I when you are
breathing
Breathe but it was us two plus exponential
feeling
Trying to hold myself up on my self but i'd
already be leaving

Somewhere

Far and close
ToFrom blue
FromTo You

My Time with Dad

All my time
with Dad
Is heaven

Dad heaven
Passes by quickly

Sights of Love

I want to take it out
Chuck it out
Throw it wet and schlumpy
Watch it whine and weep on
cold concrete

Watch it whimper and whimper and
Whimper and Whimper and
whimper
and
whimper and
I'm already crying over it.

I pick it up with singed palms and cradle it
gently
singing to it lullabies until it lulls to sleep to
Sleep with it and to wake up to
Wet and schlumpy
smoochies

Me and Bug

I stuck around for Bug
He pranced on my palm
Kissed all my fingies
Danced on my knuckles

I ate from peach yogurt
He sipped from watermelon droplets
I cooed his name
He swirled his antenna
I didn't wait to love Bug

I wrote a poem for Bug
In the middle of writing it I looked up
Found only a Heart Tug
But no loving Bug

I thought he disappeared
Continued on without me

BUT WAIT!!
He appeared
On the end
Of my pinkie!!

I stuck around for Bug

And he stuck back
"I love you Bug"
"I love you back"

Handheld

Small as a pixie
I rest in your palm
Sandwiched between
Your palms and your eyes

One Big Life hides me

I want nothing more than to use your cupped
hands as a megaphone
Magnify my voice beyond the sandwich space
Invite in other other-sized creatures

But I rest in the sandwich

Coveted

Looked At

Hidden within the Big Life

Children in the Wings of Life

All the kids are buzzing waiting
for Tomorrow

A million colors passing through hallways
Syllabus paper hot from the printer
Writing names on top right corners
Name games
New and Old names!!
Asking for Today's Date

All the kids can't sleep when
the today of the first day of the school year
is more exciting than
the tonight of the last night of the break

Church Body

I stand
Under an infinite umbrella
Protected from a dying, driving storm
If I am alive to see the Great Sky clear
Then Rejoice
If I am dead when the rain drives on

Rejoice

Wizardry Bridging Life and Death

On the stage
In the song
And then in your legacy
You speak to me
Unmistakably
I catch your winking smile in empty air

You speak to me
On the stage
In the song
And then your legacy lives on
I believe in it
As you believed in me
Unmistakably
your legacy lives on
In me

Grandma Crown

My future prophesied in familiar flesh:
Sagging flesh
Quivering fingers
Hungry eyes flashing glimpses:
A lifetime of golden experience

God sculpted a baby into a beautiful old woman
And this beautiful old woman sculpts me
forward

Scary Giant Eye and Living Gem

MOST PRECIOUS GEM
LODGED IN SCARY GIANT'S EYE
THE PRECIOUS GEM SHINES BRIGHT
LODGED IN SCARY GIANT'S EYE

A TESTAMENT THAT
SCARY GIANT SHINES TOO
THERE IN THE HOLE IS THE LAST
EVIDENCE OF HIS SHINING TRUTH

Performance Night

Creature forces his delicate heart
up against the deepest corners of his shell

Everyone out here loves him and
he is experiencing hell

Out, out, Creature
Your veins are your veins
Power is held in your play
Yet you put power into the fear
Of You being here
Of Us being near

As sure as the curtain will call
As sure as the seats will fill with attention
As sure as the fear in your heart to be seen
Convinces you that your heart must be Fortified

Your shell is delicate too
Very see-through, please believe us
We can see you.

Creature, I love you
Please believe me, I love you
But you must come out
Creature, the curtain is up

Time with Mom

Loud laughter
Tongue over teeth
Teeth on flesh
Bite mark critique

Time with mom must be
Captured
Between frequent phone calls
I stand on business
Fruitlessly listening
To her foreign exchanges

I capture her English words
In our precious time gaps
She'll buy me lunch
I'll chew on our chat

We continue on
Our motherdaughter dance
But until then
I hunt for my chance

I mean I'd like to talk with her

Tomboy Woman

I swore on my identity that i'd be defined
In a line of other tomboys like myself

I rested my head in hooded jackets
Stacked my closet with oversized t-shirts
And re-wore my real worn out sneakers
Hoping the teachers would see a tomboy
Not a girly girl with pretty princess features

Last weekend I craned my head over grandma's
hand
Ran the soft brush dipped in nail polish over her
nails
Cream colored pearl nails complimenting my
magentas
We held hands and the colors complimented
each other

Yesterday I took my clothes out the dryer and
ran out of
Hangers to hang my new mumus and summer
dresses
My new panties I bought don't mesh with my
old panties

I brought with me over the years so i'm leaving
them aside

Tomorrow I won't swear on that old identity
I'll define myself in flowery princessy delicate
definitions like
Tight-fitting T-shirts with long flowing hair tied
together with
My Woman's Features

She bursts out Lively

This seashell didn't show up on the shore
She wasn't pushed onto sand
She was hidden under the land
Didn't understand birth any more
Than the fish understand the concept of air

She was searched for long before she was due
She was waited upon long before she knew
Formed without sunlight
Carved without idea
Birthed by the will of heaven's might
She was birthed in the sea's section in the
middle of the night